Soccer Is Fun!

by Robin Nelson

first step nonfiction

Lerner Publications Company · Minneapolis

LERNER

SOURCE™

Expand learning beyond the printed book. Download free, complementary educational resources for this book from our website, www.lerneresource.com.

The images in this book are used with the permission of: © iStockphoto.com/ryasick, p. 4; © iStockphoto.com/bonnie jacobs, p. 5; © Fotokostic/Shutterstock.com, pp. 6, 14; © iStockphoto.com/mandygodbehear, p. 7; © iStockphoto.com/Sean Nel, p. 8; © iStockphoto.com/nicole abejon, p. 9; © iStockphoto.com/Phil Augustavo, p. 10; © Monkey Business Images/the Agency Collection/Getty Images, p. 11; © iStockphoto.com/LifesizeImages, p. 12; © Barry Austin Photography/Lifesize/Getty Images, p. 13; © iStockphoto.com/Michael Krinke, p. 15; © Moment/Cultura/Getty Images, p. 16; © iStockphoto.com/Amy Myers, p. 17; © iStockphoto.com/Christopher Futcher, pp. 18, 19; © Laura Westlund/Independent Picture Service, p. 21.

Front cover: © iStockphoto.com/Sergiy Serdyuk.

Main body text set in ITC Avant Garde Gothic Std Medium 21/25.
Typeface provided by Adobe Systems.

Lerner Publications Company
A division of Lerner Publishing Group, Inc.
241 First Avenue North
Minneapolis, MN 55401 U.S.A.

Website address: www.lernerbooks.com

Library of Congress Cataloging-in-Publication Data

Nelson, Robin, 1971–
    Soccer is fun! / by Robin Nelson.
        p.   cm. — (First step nonfiction—Sports are fun!)
    Includes index.
    ISBN 978–1–4677–1105–0 (lib. bdg. : alk. paper)
    ISBN 978–1–4677–1747–2 (eBook)
    1. Soccer—Juvenile literature. I. Title.
GV943.25.N45 2014
796.334—dc23   2012033863

Manufactured in the United States of America
1 – PC – 7/15/13

Table of Contents

Soccer

Do you like to run and kick a ball?

You can play soccer!

Two teams play soccer.

The team that scores the
most **goals** wins.

Soccer players wear shoes called **cleats**.

Soccer players wear **shin pads** to protect their legs.

Let's Play!

The **referee** blows the whistle.

Each team tries to get the ball into the other team's goal.

11

You can kick the ball to
move it.

You can even bounce the
ball off your head!

But you cannot use your
arms or your hands.

Only **goalkeepers** can use their hands to stop the ball.

Some players try to score.

Other players try to keep
the ball away from their
goal.

A player kicks the ball
toward the goal.

The ball goes into the goal.
The team that shot the ball
scores a point!

The Soccer Field

A soccer field has a goal on each end. The ball starts in the center of the field. There are lines around the field. The ball must stay inside these lines.

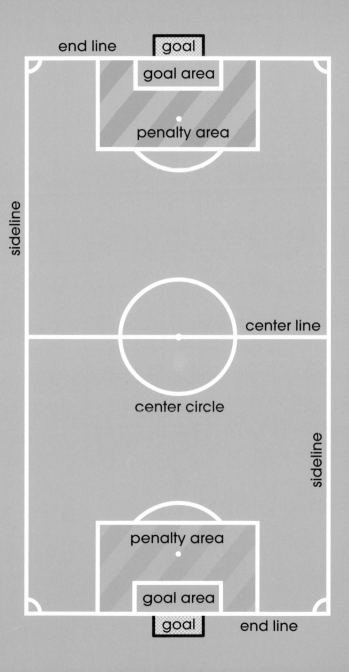

end line

goal

goal area

penalty area

sideline

center line

center circle

sideline

penalty area

goal area

goal

end line

Fun Facts

- A soccer team has 11 players. But many younger teams have fewer players.

- Soccer is the world's most popular sport.

- Only Americans call the game soccer. The rest of the world calls the game football.

- There is a lot of running in soccer. It is a great way to get exercise!

Glossary

cleats – shoes with knobs on the bottoms to keep you from sliding

goalkeepers – players who protect the goal

goals – points earned when the ball goes into the other team's goal. The word *goal* can also refer to the frame with the net that is on both ends of a soccer field.

referee – a person who makes sure the players are following the rules

shin pads – pads that you strap onto the lower part of your legs to protect them

Index